Re-reading *The Gospel of Sri Ramakrishna*

Re-reading *The Gospel of Sri Ramakrishna* in the 21st century.

TAPATI BHARADWAJ

Re-reading *The Gospel of Sri Ramakrishna*

Copyright © 2014 Tapati Bharadwaj

All rights reserved.

ISBN: 8192875237
ISBN-13: 978-8192875231

DEDICATION

To Hope, that we, in India, allow ourselves more intellectual space to think beyond within the domain of Hinduism.

Re-reading *The Gospel of Sri Ramakrishna*

CONTENTS

	Acknowledgments	i
1	Introduction	1
2	Being	6
3	Civilizational Changes	10
4	Gender Doesn't Matter	14
5	Devotion as Performance	19
6	Conclusion: Rammohun Roy	22

Re-reading *The Gospel of Sri Ramakrishna*

ACKNOWLEDGMENTS

The city of Calcutta is mesmerizing because of its polyphonic nature. As we tread our way through a text that is also carnivalesque in nature and refuses to be contained within a single interpretative matrix, we realize on the impossibility of arriving at any overarching truth.

Re-reading *The Gospel of Sri Ramakrishna*

1 INTRODUCTION

In another twelve years, Sri Ramakrishna would be two hundred years old. That we still read *The Gospel of Sri Ramakrishna*,[1] and find meaning in most of what he said, despite living in social conditions that are extremely different from how they were when he was alive – does say a lot about him. How do we interpret what he said? – when specially much of what he did say was, at face value, socially relevant only in mid-late nineteenth century India.

We, in urban India, belong to a generation that is flippant in our habits and our notions of Indian-ness, flirt with global cultures and the colonial past is a distant dream. And yet, *The Gospel* does make sense. One can imagine Sri Ramakrishna, examining us benevolently, and questioning us about our lifestyles; never judging us but engaging with us and having a discussion, so that we ourselves are critically empowered to understand ourselves better.

Sri Ramakrishna is obviously enough, not specific to any particular nation or community or religious belief. He embraces all and in this all embracing gesture, reaches out to everyone. His teachings critique the global dominant notion that we have about mainstream Hinduism – where Indian-ness and being Hindu is equated with a repressive concept of moral prudishness.

The endeavor here is to read *The Gospel of Sri Ramakrishna* and derive meaning in a manner that it relates to our lives in a global world culture. Our world, at the present, is akin to the multicultural, polyphonic city of Calcutta as it was in the nineteenth century. We tend to forget this. In fact, it would be a meaningful exercise if we positioned Sri Ramakrishna within the larger socio-cultural context of nineteenth century Calcutta.

The long nineteenth century in India saw the emergence of the

---

[1] *The Gospel of Sri Ramakrishna* (Abridged) by Swami Nikhilananda.

East India Company as rulers of India and the gradual transformation of the city as many aspects of western civilization were imported bag and baggage into the country. For example, at the turn of the century, books made their way into Indian society and displaced a manuscript culture. Natives started to read, make use of and negotiate their lives through printed texts. Moreover, the press initiated a shift in the very nature of how texts were to be written, preserved and disseminated. In fact, it initiated a shift in the very method of writing, a shift that involved cultural habits – Indians would sit on the floor and write, unlike Europeans who used tables and chairs. Nathaniel Halhed[2] describes it in the following manner: "As they have neither chairs nor tables, their posture in writing is very different from ours: they sit upon their heels, or sometimes upon their hams, while their left hand held open serves as a desk whereon to lay the paper on which they write, which is kept in its place by the thumb: so that they never write on a large sheet of paper without folding it down to a very small surface"[3] It is fascinating to conjecture as to how exactly the change to print took place. As more and more natives had access to printed texts, that which had been the privilege of a particular class of people, now became democratized. Now, a large canvas of Indian society had access to printed books. How did it feel to be able to touch printed paper and read, and be aware that many others across the land were also reading the same text? Indians closely interacted with the Britishers and learnt their social manners, learning how the technology worked. They also learnt the different uses that print could come into.

The "white" city of Calcutta, in the nineteenth century, also developed in a distinct manner. By the end of the eighteenth century, trade from Bengal comprised a large percentage of the goods sent to Europe and Calcutta as its port grew in importance to become the commercial and administrative center of the British empire. As the white residents had very little contact with the natives, could not own land outside Calcutta, and lived under the strict control of the Company, a semi-isolated colonial realm-city was created. All the civic, socio-architectural and cultural institutions of England were imported and in the process, the architectural landscape of the city was changed.[4] Writing in the early nineteenth century,

---

[2] Nathaniel Halhed, *A Grammar of the Bengal Language*. 1778. Reprint, ed. R. C. Alston (England: The Scolar Press, 1969).

[3] Nathaniel Halhed, *A Grammar of the Bengal Language*, p. 2.

[4] William Kuiters, *The British in Bengal, 1756-1773. A Society in Transition Seen through the Biography of a Rebel: William Bolts (1739-1808)* (Paris: Les Indes Savante, 2002), pp. 23-62.

Viscount George Valentia described Calcutta as "well worthy of being the seat of our Eastern Government, both from its size, and from the magnificent buildings which decorate the part of it inhabited by Europeans."[5]

Colonial territorial power was made evident through a visual display of spectacle where the architectural presence of buildings created an aura of imperial separation, wealth and British superiority. The realm of a western city created and enabled the establishment of a socio-imperial identity in Calcutta, intrinsic to maintaining a colonial territory

This world was peripheral in Sri Ramakrishna's life, but he was aware of the multiple worlds that existed side by side in the city of Calcutta. It is important to remember this fact as an important subtext of *The Gospel*.

The "unstable" text: *The Gospel* as an unstable text.

The Gospel is not necessarily a completely stable text; it is full of self-contradictory statements and as readers, we are at a loss. Sri Ramakrishna would not have wanted his words to be codified and it is almost as if he was cautioning us against us and his disciples to arrive at grand overarching Truths. His words, therefore, cannot be translated into the printed form and in the process of doing so, the printed text of *The Gospel*, has become unstable.

Let us consider the following incident from *The Gospel*: it is a well known fact that the family of Rani Rashmoni was intimately connected with the Britishers as their fortune depended on them. It would have been usual and not out of the norm for them to socialize with them also. But there is an incident in *The Gospel* where an explanatory footnote comments that it would have been taboo for Hindus to be on familiar terms with the Britishers.

> Master (to the other devotees): "Captain [a devotee] forbids me to go to see Keshab [of the Brahmo Samaj]."

---

[5] Viscount George Valencia, "Calcutta in 1803." in *Calcutta in the Nineteenth Century*. ed. Thankappan Nair (Calcutta: Firma KLM, 1999), pp. 1-35; p. 11. He goes on to say: "The sums expended upon [the city] have been considered as extravagant by those who carry European ideas and European economy into Asia; but they ought to remember, that India, us a country of splendor, of extravagance, and of outward appearances: that the Head of a mighty empire ought to conform himself to the prejudices of the country he rules over." p. 12.

Captain: "But, sir, you act as you will. What can I do?"

Master (sharply): "Why should'nt I go to see Keshab? You feel at ease when you go to the Governor General's house and for money at that. Keshab thinks of God and chants His name. ...Doesn't God dwell in Kehshab also?"

With those words the Master left the room abruptly and went to the northeast verandah."[6]

Footnote to the Captain's visits to the Governor General's house: "According to orthodox Hindu custom, an Englishman is a *mlechcha*, one outside the pale of Hindu society. The touch of a *mlechcha* pollutes a Hindu."

If we closely examine what happened, we will realize that Sri Ramakrishna was unhappy at being told whom to visit and whom not to; he wanted to visit Keshab and did not like that the Captain was cautioning him against it. The footnote (which is a later on addition) explains the Captain's visits to the house of the British Governor General as unbecoming of a Hindu. The implication is that Sri Ramakrishna did not approve of the Captain socializing with the Britishers, and yet he allowed him so. (And on similar grounds, the Captain should allow him to visit Keshab.) But we wonder – would Sri Ramakrishna have had such dichotomous feelings towards the Britishers, considering how well he know the workings of the family of Rani Rashmoni. Is meaning in this particular instance an interpolation of the editor, that does not reflect what Sri Ramakrishna has to say?

How do we then, derive meaning from a text that has the potential to be "unstable"? The instability arises when we project our concerns, likes and dislikes, and moral notions into the written text of *The Gospel*, and in the process, elide what Sri Ramakrishna really meant.

The text as a conundrum.

The Gospel of Sri Ramakrishna has an a-historical appeal that cuts across generations, time periods, geo-social spaces and lifestyle choices. The text

---

[66] *The Gospel*, p. 278.

or the person is not the sole belonging of a particular institution or a group of people.

More often than not, Sri Ramakrishna spoke in riddles, and his sayings are self contradictory, on the verge of being unsolved conundrums – as if questioning the intelligence of the listener. His guise of an unlettered rustic, poor Brahmin helped him. As a reader, we can be thrown off the track if we fall into that trap.

From *The Gospel*:

> Narendra said to M. that he had been reading a book by Hamilton, who wrote: "A legend is the end of philosophy and the beginning of religion."
>
> Master (to M.): "What does that mean?"
>
> Narendra explained the sentence in Bengali. The Master beamed with joy and said in English, "Thank you! Thank you!" Everyone laughed at the charming way he said these words. They knew that his English vocabulary consisted of only half a dozen words.

Sri Ramakrishna allowed himself to negate his position of privilege as a teacher and enabled the student to teach him and in the process, established a non-hierarchical relationship. The Master "beamed with joy" – at the fact that Vivekananda was able to make a linguistic-epistemic shift.

The more we allow ourselves to delve into *The Gospel*, we realize that we can engage with the text as a literary masterpiece.

2 BEING

There is a tendency to often misunderstand what Sri Ramakrishna had to say about charity; namely that compassion and charity (philanthropy, in other words) should be given to others without a desire to spread one's fame and glory. It is a reductive exercise if we give only because we want to be known as great for our kindness. The act of being, in other words, is that we give anonymously – like an anonymous donor – without really thinking that we would attain great fame subsequently.

If we look at the following incident from *The Gospel*, this notion becomes clearer:

> Master: "… People who carry to excess the giving of alms, or the distributing of food among the poor, fall victims to the desire of acquiring name and fame."

> "Sambhu Mitra once talked about establishing hospitals, dispensaries, and schools, making roads, digging public reservoirs, and so forth. I said to him: 'Don't go out of your way to look for such works. Undertake only those works that present themselves to you and are of pressing necessity and those also in a spirit of detachment." It is not good to become involved in many activities. That makes one forget God."[7]

This is an extremely difficult task; Sri Ramakrishna was talking about leading a balanced life and cautioning against "excesses". Philanthropy is but one aspect of our whole existence where we live as social beings. We also hesitate to be made invisible; for in such social exercises, in giving and sharing, do we expect some form of social reciprocity. Sri Ramakrishna was cautioning us against expecting such kinds of "returns" in any kind through

---

[7] Ibid., p. 142.

our acts of charity, and instead be in a state of Being where we were always kind and charitable.

Undoing caste and gender hierarchies.

The *Gospel Of Sri Ramakrishna* reveals a man who was, more than anything else, absolutely kind and loving towards all around him. He was a teacher, at the crossroads of the long nineteenth century, but amalgamating different world views. Socio-cultural, epistemic and technological changes had taken place in the city of Calcutta that was gradually embracing many things from the west. A pre colonial civilization was face on with the juggernaut of changes from the West. As a teacher, Sri Ramakrishna reconciled different civilizational perspectives, thereby bringing to the forefront the politics of his position, akin to what we would call a standpoint theory.

There are many instances in his life, when he undid his social privilege, and by doing so, was able to empathize with the Other. During his thread ceremony when he was nine, he accepted a cooked meal by his nurse, a *sudra* woman. This was quite out of keeping for a brahmanical family. By doing so, he undid his position of privilege as a Brahmin.

Sri Ramakrishna was unable to separate the self from the Other; the Other was always a part of himself. This process of absolute identification allowed him greater insight and empathy into how the Other lived. He was intimate with his disciples; but he was equally intimate and affectionate with those at the lower most rungs of society. The following incident makes that clear:

> Rasik was a sweeper of the Kali temple, who lived in Dakshineshwar. One day I heard the Master talking with him in the latter's courtyard. They were talking very intimately, as though they were close friends.[8]

The enormous capacity to negate the self and identify with the most oppressed is what makes Sri Ramakrishna extremely attractive as a person. At a time period, when female actresses were seen as prostitutes, and their reputation was construed as being morally questionable, Sri

---

[8] From Kedar Nath Bandopadhyay's account on Sri Ramakrishna in *Ramakrishna as we saw Him*, by Swami Chetananda (Kolkata: Advaita Ashram, 2008), pp. 365-370.

Ramakrishna did not hesitate to make parallels between his life as a teacher who reaches across to all, irrespective of religious beliefs, and a "public women" who makes herself available to all.

Sri Ramakrishna wanted Shivanath Shastri to visit him but he was unable to do so because of work at the Brahmo Samaj. Sri Ramakrishna personally visited him, despite his new disciples asking him not to as a Brahmo was not "worth it."[9] In reply Sri Ramakrishna said:

> Now look here! One who has publicly registered her name goes to all, whoever seeks her [referring to the custom then prevalent of all public women registering their names before commencing their profession]. I am at the service of all.[10]

Shivanath Shastri's brief account on Sri Ramakrishna in *Ramakrishna as we saw Him* is quite revealing in how he, and the Brahmo Samaj, viewed the theatre; as being filled with "objectionable characters" who were also his disciples.[11]

Sri Ramakrishna looked at the fact that the actresses comprised a group of socially disenfranchised women, who earned a living by being in the theatre in performing arts. He supported women who were in the public realm, and who were socially conscribed to be marginalised on social-moral grounds. This act of solidarity undid dominant norms of gender roles; why else would Sri Ramakrishna refer to his act of a teacher who visits all indiscriminately as being akin to that of a "public" woman who was available to all. By doing so, he undid his socio-cultural position as a teacher who was privileged to have great knowledge.

---

[9] Ibid., p. 398.

[10] Ibid., p. 399.

[11] Ibid., p. 399.

Sri Ramakrishna as a feminist

The *Gospel of Sri Ramakrishna* has to be interpreted as a literary text. If we strive to arrive at literal meanings, we will only be face to face with riddles and obtain an extremely simplistic and reductive perspective on Sri Ramakrishna. The reader will be reducing him to a flat figured, mono-dimensional persona and the truth about him was far from this.

The fact that we never hear an outright statement by Sri Ramakrishna on whether women in India were oppressed and needed to be empowered or so on, makes us conclude that he did not have anything to contribute to this debate which was quite a dominant theme in the long nineteenth century in India. The truth was actually far from this. The conundrum, therefore, becomes this: how do we derive meaning from silences?

If we read an incident from *The Gospel*, the meaning of such kinds of silences becomes clear.

> Surendra's (a devotee) Brother: "The Brahmo Samaj preaches the freedom of women and the abolition of the caste system. What do you think about these matters?"
>
> Master: "Men feel that way when they are just beginning to develop spiritual yearnings." [And he goes on to talk about spiritual detachment and completely avoids answering the question.][12]

What are we to make out of such kinds of silences? Sri Ramakrishna was a feminist. We realize that he never did answer directly but he did answer the question in a different manner. He does make it clear that there was a correlation between spiritual development and the capacity to do away with socio-cultural hierarchies. His answer that men would want to empower women as a result of their spiritual development is not exactly an easy concept to grasp, but he does point out to the fact that social development was but a part of the spiritual growth in a society.

---

[12] *The Gospel*, p. 157.

3 CIVILIZATIONAL CHANGES

For some unknown reason, the dominant common perception on Sri Ramakrishna is that he eschewed westernization and espoused a going-back-to-the-roots philosophy. But was he really so anti-change? The city of Calcutta (and India) underwent major socio-cultural, economical and technological changes as a result of the presence of the East India Company and the Britishers over the long nineteenth century as many aspects of western civilization were imported. If we consider the following incident from his life, we are given an insight into how he viewed these changes that were taking place.

Sri Ramakrishna and his disciples were on a boat trip with Keshab Sen (of the Brahmo Samaj) and his disciples. After the boat docked, they went for a ride through the city. From *The Gospel*:

> The carriage drove through the European quarter of the city. The Master enjoyed the sight of the beautiful mansions on both sides of the well lighted streets. Suddenly he said: "I am thirsty. What's to be done?" Nandalal, Keshab's nephew, stopped the carriage before the India Club and went upstairs to get some water. The Master inquired whether the glass had been well washed. On being assured that it had been, he drank the water.

> As the carriage went along, the Master put his head out of the window and looked with childlike enjoyment at the people, the vehicles, the horses, and the streets, all flooded with moonlight. Now and then he heard European ladies singing at the piano. He was in a very happy mood.[13]

---

[13] Ibid., p. 143.

There is a correlation between the Master's "happy mood" and the environment – which reflects the western parts of Calcutta. It was as if he was appreciating the changing nature of the city; stasis for Sri Ramakrishna was abhorrent. But not all change was inevitable good or desirable. It was as if he was acknowledging that certain aspects of western civilization did do good for India and the question to ask is this: how did he conceptualize of change?

Zamindars.

Sri Ramakrishna was all inclusive to the point where he embraced the poor as well as the rich, the religious and the drunkard, the prostitute as well as the hermit. That was incredibly kind of him. Here is an instance from *The Gospel*:

> "I visited my father-in-law's house. They arranged a *kirtan*. It was a great religious festival, and there was much singing of God's holy name. Now and then I would wonder about my future. I would say to the Divine Mother, "Mother, I shall take my spiritual experiences to be real if the landlords of the country show me respect." They too came of their own accord and talked with me."[14]

Did he really want the rich and wealthy to come and pay obeisance to him or was he just acting out a role – namely, that of an unlettered Brahmin of humble means, who had grown up in rural Bengal. Playing this role meant that he would have to embrace the accolades handed out to him by the rich, even if he really did not care much about them. In most ways, he was jesting (and being funny) about social expectations. More importantly, at a time period when the landed gentry was gradually becoming westernized (as colonial rule continued through the long nineteenth century), Sri Ramakrishna was reminding the "landlords" that India did have a history before the presence of the East India Company as rulers.

Sri Ramakrishna's childhood was very similar to Vidyasagar's younger days, as both came from humble, brahmanical families from rural Bengal. When Sri Ramakrishna went to visit him, Vidyasagar was someone who had blended certain aspects of the West into his brahmanical lifestyle and belief system. Maybe, this was a civilizational amalgamation that Sri

---

[14] *The Gospel*, p. 131-132.

Ramakrishna could understand and would have wanted India to aspire towards.

The following incident from *The Gospel* makes that clear:

> He lived in a two-storey house, built in the English fashion, with lawns on all sides and surrounded by a high wall. After climbing the stairs to the second floor, Sri Ramakrishna and his devotees entered a room at the far end of which Vidyasagar was seated facing them, with a table in front of him. To the right of the table was a bench....
>
> Vidyasagar rose to receive the Master. Sri Ramakrishna stood in front of the bench, with one hand resting on the table. He gazed at Vidyasagar, as if they had known each other before and smiled in an ecstatic mood.
>
> ... Sri Ramakrishna, still in an ecstatic mood, sat on the bench....
>
> Sri Ramakrishna said: "Your activities are inspired by *sattva*. Though they are *rajasic*, they are influenced by *sattva*. Compassion springs from *sattva*. ... You are distributing food and learning, that is good too. If these activities are done in a selfless spirit they lead to God. But most people work for fame or to acquire merit. Their activities are not selfless."[15]

Vidyasagar's enormous capacity to be charitable was not for personal gains or fame and this has to be the moot focus of any action. Subsequently, when Swami Vivekananda would establish the Ramakrishna Mission, this notion of "compassion towards all" would be, and is, the determining factor of the Mission's activities.

Daya/ Maya

Sri Ramakrishna was all encompassing in his love towards mankind; at a time period, which is post 1857 when India had already fought its first war of Independence against colonial rule, he propounded an attitude which implied that even the Britishers had something which had benefited us as a nation.

---

[15] Ibid., pp.100-101.

From *The Gospel*:

> To love these [family] objects, regarding them as one's own, is *maya*. But to love all things is *daya*, compassion. To love only the members of the Brahmo Samaj or of one's own family is *maya*; to love one's own countrymen is *maya*. But to love the people of all countries, to love the members of all religions, is *daya*. Such love comes from God, from *daya*.
>
> ...
>
> Again the conversation turned to the English people. A devotee said, "Sir, I understand that nowadays the pundits of England do not believe in the existence of God."
>
> ...
>
> Master: "Well, that is enough. They believe in Shakti, don't they? Then why should they be atheists?"[16]

It is not really clear as to why he would hesitate to condemn the Britishers; but if we consider *daya* as being a fundamental aspect of our being, it does become comprehensible as to why we should be willing to engage with a global world. This statement speaks volumes on Sri Ramakrishna's worldview. Why would we want to care for others? Sri Ramakrishna explained the concept to his disciples within the framework of religion; the Britishers believed in Shakti which did make them religious. It did not matter that they were not Hindus. It would do us good to keep this view in mind in our present global world, which is divided on grounds of culture and religion.

---

[16] Ibid., pp. 456-457.

4 GENDER DOES'NT MATTER

Often when we read *The Gospel*, we come across statements which, on the face of it, are absolutely misogynous and ridiculously ridden with machoism. For example, what are we to make of the following advice given by Sri Ramakrishna:

> You must be extremely careful about women. Women speak of the attitude of Gopala! Pay no attention to such things. The proverb says: 'A woman devours the three worlds.' Many women, when they see handsome and healthy young men, lay snares for them. That is what they call the 'attitude of Gopala.'[17]

If we read such advice at the literal level, we are idiots.

In *The Gospel*, Sri Ramakrishna used events from everyday life to clarify the absolute Truth; it made it easier for most to understand him. The instances that he drew up were within the socio-cultural context of nineteenth century Bengal and cannot be construed in a trans-historical manner; they were specific to that time period.

Sri Ramakrishna would have been aware of the socio-legal changes that were taking place and affecting all aspects of society. He would have been aware that women were in a fragile position within society and were often abused.

He would also have been cognizant of the changing realm of the domestic as printed texts were imported from England and consumed by the masses. Sri Ramakrishna was extremely critical of these emergent notions of bourgeois domesticity and this translated into his caution against "women."

---

[17] Ibid., p. 603.

In *Domesticity in Colonial India: What Women Learned When Men Gave Them Advice*,[18] we learn how notions of bourgeois domesticity were disseminated within the larger public sphere in Bengal through Bengali tracts that were written in the second half of the nineteenth century. Bourgeois, European ideas on home and the family were consumed by the educated, upwardly mobile social groups of colonial Bengal. What emerged were new notions of conjugal love, intimacy and heterosexual coupledom which were seen as more attractive in contrast to subservience to elder female guardians. English-educated *bhadralok* men in and around Calcutta translated their newly learned ideas of romance, and domesticity, into vernacular manuals of advice, letters, imagined conversations and novels.

Sri Ramarkrishna saw such social changes from the west as being detrimental in allowing men and women from leading lives that were more diverse and inclusive and outside the model of bourgeois domesticity. He was not really against romance but he wanted women and men to engage with the world on all levels, which would include the spiritual, the social and the worldly.

"kamini" and "kanchan"

Was Sri Ramakrishna a misogynist? – considering the endless number of times he reiterated the dictum that those who aspire for a higher truth should eschew *kamini-kanchan* which loosely translates into renouncing one's desires for "women and gold." But is there any compulsion to make a literal translation of this reference? What I would like to propose, instead, is that we understand Sri Ramakrishna's sayings in a more non-literal, symbolic manner, as doing so, will allow us to have a greater understanding of what he actually meant. After all, he was quite pro-woman, and advocated the empowerment of the most oppressed.

If we position Sri Ramakrishna within his time period and try to locate him within other forms of mainstream Hinduism, we will see that he was an anomaly of sorts. Apart from brahmo-ism and Keshav Sen with whom Ramakrishna interacted quite intimately, what was the nature of other aspects of Hinduism perceived by most? We get an inkling when we read what Tanika Sarkar in *Hindu Wife, Hindu Nation, Community, Religion and Cultural Nationalism*[19] has to say about Tarakeshwar, a rich and popular

---

[18] By Judith E. Walsh and Maryland Lanham (Maryland: Rowman & Littlefield Publishers, 2004)

[19] Published by Indian University Press, 2010.

Saivite pilgrimage place in Hoogly; that it was a "centre of great [sexual] scandals, at least from the early nineteenth century."[20] In 1824, mohunt Srimata Giri received the death sentence for murdering the lover of his mistress.[21] This event did not receive much public attention as did the one that took place fifty years later, largely a result of the dissemination of printed texts and the presence of a print-induced public sphere.

Tanika Sarkar succinctly refers to certain social events which were of great importance in the psyche of the Bengali public. In 1873, a powerful mohunt, Madhav Chandra Giri, of Tarakeshwar, who was the manager-cum-guru, was accused of "seducing" and "raping" Elokeshi, the young wife of one Nobinchandra Banerjee, an employee at a military press in Calcutta. Elokeshi was killed by her husband in a moment of anger and subsequently, a trial was set up in the Calcutta court. This event attracted the attention of people all across. Nobinchandra was pardoned, as a result of public demands for mercy, while the mohunt, who was represented by an English lawyer, was fined 3000 rupees. The Bengali public was unhappy with this judicial discussion, and a harsher sentence was demanded for the mohunt.

The "moral health" of the Hindu religious leadership received critical attention from the early 1860's by reformist journalists who looked at the sexual misconduct of the powerful Ballabhacharya sect of western India.[22] It is within this context, where mainstream Hinduism was associated with certain forms of sexual excesses, that we have to understand the nature of Sri Ramakrishna'a dictum to eschew *kamini-kanchan*.

I use the above account as a way to introduce the main issue – how did Sri Ramakrishna negotiate with and against the socio-cultural and legal changes that were taking place in the long nineteenth century? *The Gospel of Sri Ramakrishna* has to be understood within this context.

---

[20] Ibid., p. 580.

[21] Ibid., p. 58.

[22] Ibid., p. 62.

In Solidarity with the oppressed.

What is a remarkable fact and glossed over is that Sri Ramakrishna, during his lifetime, identified with one of the most oppressed groups and displayed a great degree of solidarity. Actresses were seen as "fallen" women – a social construct that they themselves internalized.

An incident from *The Gospel*:

> After the theatre, the actresses, following Girish's instructions, came to the room to salute Sri Ramakrishna. They bowed before him, touching the ground with their foreheads. ...
>
> After the actresses had left the room, Sri Ramakrishna said to the devotees, "It is all He, only in different forms."[23]

By visiting the theatre and blessing all involved, Sri Ramakrishna desired to undo these social constructs where identity is predetermined by one's labor and for these women who had no form of income but through acting.

One of the most well known actresses of the Bengali theatre was Binodini dasi and she was born in 1863. She grew up without a father; her grandmother and mother had a small house and some cottages which they leased out and this rent was their sole income. When she was six years old, her younger brother of five years age was married to an orphan of two and half years and this child brought some jewelry as dowry that she had inherited from her mother. Eventually, even this was sold off as the family was incredibly poor. Her brother died quite young, leaving her family quite devastated. Binodini got admission to a free school where she learnt how to read and write and speak a little English. When she was nine, a young woman named Gangamani moved into their house as a tenant; she would become a singer and actress in the Star Theatre and was considered family.

Eventually, Binodini was encouraged to join the theatre; she was told that in the initial years, she would receive pocket money and subsequently, would earn a generous salary.

In her story, *Amar Katha*, Binodini refers to herself as a "fallen woman" – and this was how society viewed her. When Sri Ramakrishna

---

[23] Ibid., p. 683.

blessed her, she wrote: "I can't express how his beautiful, loving, compassionate gaze fell on a lowly person like me!"

How does it feel for one to define the self as a "lowly person"? This kind of self-debasement would have been incredibly humiliating for these actresses. Sri Ramakrishna did understand the extent to which they were marginalized within mainstream Hindu society in the nineteenth century and by aligning himself with them, he aimed towards undoing their social oppression.

5 DEVOTION AS PERFORMANCE

Standpoint Theory

We are really unable to understand the extent to which Sri Ramakrishna went in order to identify with the Other. In what can but be described, in present day terms, as anthropological surveys, he would live life as the Other to engage with how s/he lived. How does it feel to be a woman? – the best way would be to live life like a woman. Usually, gender norms are socially prescribed in an extremely dichotomous fashion, and we cannot fathom why Sri Ramakrihsn would "regard" himself as the "handmaid of the Divine Mother." We consider this kind of shifting across gender roles as subversive. We fail to understand that this was but a strategy he used to understand lives from the Other's point of view.

From *The Gospel*:

> "At that time I was almost unconscious of the outer world. Mathur Babu kept me at his Janbazar mansion a few days. While living there I regarded myself as the handmaid of the Divine Mother. The ladies of the house didn't feel at all bashful with me. They felt as free before me as women feel before a small boy or girl. I used to escort Mathur's daughter to her husband's chamber with the maidservant."[24]

This, indeed, was quite a performance where even the women of the *andarmahal* were quite comfortable and did not feel awkward in his presence. Was it needed for Sri Ramakrishna to efface himself? These instances reveal the extent to which he went in order to identify with the Other; doing so allowed him to look at life from the lived reality of another's perspective.

---

[24] *The Gospel*, pp. 231-232.

Devotion as Performance.

Sri Ramakrishna could identify with the suffering of Others, and sometimes, he would enact how the Other lived/ was in order to fully comprehend and grasp life from his/her viewpoint. The capacity to do so – performatively live life like the Other – was a result of his ability to efface the self and be an actor in real life.

Some incidents from his childhood are quite remarkable as they recur over and over again later in his life. One incident is noteworthy: one *shivaratri*, a dramatic performance was arranged and the boy who was to play the role of Shiva fell sick; Sri Ramakrishna had to fill in his role. And he did do a stellar performance and the audience was moved.

He also arranged for a dramatic club and his friends joined him; the stage was the mango orchard and they would enact scenes from the stories of the *Ramayana* and the *Mahabharata*. His favourite theme was the Vrindaban episodes of Krishna's life; he could play the parts of Radha and Krishna.[25]

In *Ramakrishna as we saw Him*, Shivanath Shastri mentions on how Sri Ramakrishna would enact the role of the perfect devotee to understand what devotion was.

> Ramakrishna had earnestly resolved to practise what the visiting mendicants had taught him. For instance, one sage had told him that the best way to cultivate the spirit of Hanuman, the famous monkey servant of Rama, as delineated in the *Ramayana*. In order to cultivate that spirit, Ramakrishna shut himself in a room for a number of days and meditated on the virtues of Hanuman. He jumped in the room saying, "Lord, Lord, I am thy devoted servant."[26]

It did not suffice to simply read the fact that Hanuman was a great devotee and understand it intellectually; one had to also perform what it meant to be a devotee like Hanuman and live like him. Doing so, allowed Sri Ramakrishna greater authority to talk about absolute devotion.

---

[25] *The Gospel*, "Introduction," p. 5.

[26] In *Ramakrishna as we saw Him*, p. 393.

Worship and the Brahmo Samaj.

Sri Ramakrishna was quite attached to the Brahmo Samaj in many ways. Here, he was introduced to a new kind of worship, with its own order and rituals and the whole process would have interested him immensely.

From *The Gospel*:

> The Master had come to Calcutta. In the evening, he went to the house of Rajmohan, a member of the Brahmo Samaj, where Narendra and some of his young friends used to meet and worship according to the Brahmo ceremonies. Sri Ramakrishna wanted to see their worship.
>
> The Master was very happy to see Narendra and expressed a desire to watch the young men at their worship.[27]

Here, we learn that lay people were participants in the evening prayers. Sri Ramakrishna must have been moved by the fact that all, irrespective of caste and creed and gender, were involved in the prayers. More importantly, those engaged in this ceremony, were educated and there was no sense of "otherness" attached to people who performed dance or music to the deity. This sense of egalitarianism must have been an extremely attractive facet of the Brahmo Samaj.

---

[27] *The Gospel*, p. 156.

6 CONCLUSION: LOCATING THE GOSPEL WITHIN A HISTORY: VEDANTIC TRANSLATIONS AND RAMMOHUN ROY.

In *The Gospel*, we learn that Sri Ramakrishna interacted quite intimately with the Brahmo Samaj. It is of relevance that we learn more on the origins of the Brahmo Samaj and accept the fact that earlier in the nineteenth century, revisionist interpretations of Hinduism had emerged to combat the Christian missionaries. Doing so allows us to understand the larger socio-religious changes within which Sri Ramakrishna lived and worked.

Rammohun Roy, before him, had engaged with the Britishers and disseminated on Hinduism by printing texts for a global audience.

Rammohun Roy.

In the first two decades of the nineteenth century, Rammohun worked on translating the Vedantic texts. In 1815, he translated the Vedas into Bengali; in 1816-1817, he wrote the *Abridgement of the Vedanta* in English, Bengali and Hindusthani, and translated the Upanishads into English and Bengali.[28] Rammohun was supremely aware of his readership, and must have considered himself as an astute writer, churning out Bengali and English translations with great rapidity. He was able to move between different "publics". About this period of activity, he wrote:

> I have found the doctrines of Christ more conducive to moral principles, and better adapted for the use of rational beings, than any others ... and have also found Hindus in general more superstitious and miserable, both in performance of their religious rites and in their domestic concerns, than the rest of the known nations on the earth; I therefore, ... translated their most revered theological work, namely Vedant, into Bengali and Hindusthani, and

---

[28] For more on this period of activity (1815-1820), see Sophia Dobson Collet, *The Life and Letters of Raja Rammohun Roy* ed. Dilip Kumar Biswas and Prabhat Chandra Ganguli. (Calcutta: Sadharon Brahmo Samaj, 1900). Reprint 1988. pp. 60-117.

> also several chapters of the Ved... I however, in the beginnings of my pursuit, met with the greatest of opposition from their self interested leaders, the Brahmins, and was deserted by my nearest relations; I consequently felt extremely melancholy; in that critical situation, the only comfort that I had was the consoling and rational conversation of European friends, specially those in England and Scotland.[29]

The realm of readers for his English works comprised Europeans; no natives before him had written for such a readership, and therefore, there was no precedence as to what was expected from him as a native writer, writing in English for the Europeans. He was not hesitant in condemning the Brahmins, referring to them in the third person and in the process separating himself from the community of Hindus, and even voicing appreciation at how he had been received by the Europeans. In most ways, he was a native cultural mediator, making the east and his own culture comprehensible to the European reader.

His English works on the Vedanta are as follows: *Translation of an Abridgement of the Vedanta (1816), Translation of the Kena Upanishad (1816), Translation of the Isopanishad (1816), Translation of the Mundaka Upanishad (1819), Translation of the Katha Upanishad (1819)*. It is interesting to speculate on the need for such translations as the English-speaking world would already have been familiar with the Vedantic works of William Jones. In the preface to the *Translation of the Kuth Opunishud of the Ujoor Veda*,[30] Rammohun makes it very clear as to why he wrote these translations:

> I had some time ago the satisfaction of publishing a translation of the Katha-Upanishad of the Yajur-veda into Bengalee; and of distributing copies of it as widely as my circumstances would allow for the purposes of diffusing Hindoo scriptural knowledge among the adherents of that religion. The present publication is intended to assist the European community in forming their opinion respecting Hindoo Theology.[31]

---

[29] "Letter to John Digby, written in 1816", Ibid., pp. 78-79.

[30] "Preface to the Translation of the Kuth-Opunishud of the Ujoor Ved", in *The English Works of Raja Rammohun Roy. Part II*. ed. Kalidasa Nag and Debajyoti Burman (Calcutta: Sadharon Brahmo Samaj, 1946), pp. 21-38.

[31] Ibid., p. 23.

This statement is revealing, drawing attention to the nature of print in its early years, and how Rammohun made use of the power of print. William Jones and the scholars of the East India Company had worked with Hindu pandits in explaining the nature of eastern religion to the west; the Baptist missionaries had also spread their version of Hinduism by deriding it.[32] Rammohun wanted to combat these renditions of Hinduism. As we unwrap Rammohun's comment on why he had published these translations, we learn about the nature of his intended English and native readership, and the reasons why his works were important. First of all, he makes it clear that his native, Bengali reading readers were not well versed in Hinduism; therefore, he made use of a strategy that was quite expensive and he must have picked up from the missionaries—free distribution of pamphlets among the Bengali speaking Hindus so that they could improve their "scriptural knowledge". The missionaries were busy doing something similar and were also disseminating tracts in Bengali, but their focus was on ridiculing Hindu practices. The missionaries described Hinduism as originating from the devil,[33] and Rammohun, on the other hand, proclaimed that his agenda was on teaching scriptural Hinduism to the Hindus. On the other hand, the English translations were meant for the Europeans who would to some degree have been familiar with the translations of William Jones' version of Hinduism. Rammohun was a native, explaining his own religious systems to the Europeans and his credibility lay in this fact. He was almost a *pandit* who was well versed in the ways of the Europeans and made sense of the new systemic and institutional changes that were taking place.

Rammohun took it upon himself to educate his European friends about Hinduism, using phrases and a terminology that was similar to Christianity. Hindu *pandits* had assisted the East India Company scholars in their translations, but were never accorded the same kind of relevance as were the scholars of the Company. This lacuna was filled up by Rammohun who ensured that the works of natives were well acknowledged and publicised. In fact, he was so conscious of his English readership that he defined Hinduism as it was perceived by the Orientalist scholars. Sushoban Sarkar makes a similar case when he argues that the religion Rammohun formed, Brahmo-ism, also was largely elitist and never a popular religion as it failed to link up with the popular lower-caste monotheistic cults" that were numerous in eighteenth century Bengal, particularly in Nadia-

---

[32] For more see Collet, *Life and Letters*, p. 146.

[33] Ibid., p. 146.

Murshidabad.[34]

Rammohun's translations: early 19th century Calcutta

Rammohun's Vedantic works can be described as the first Vedantic commentaries in a vernacular that were written for a non Hindu, non Sanskrit speaking readership.[35] He was aware of this as draws attention to this fact in *A Defence of Hindoo Theism*, "I must remark, however, that there is no translation of the Vedas into any of the modern languages of Hindoostan with which I am acquainted."[36] His works are exegeses on the commentaries of Shankacharya and have a precedence in Baladeva Bidyubhusan's *Govindabhasya* and *Isabhasya*, which were the first Bengali commentaries that were written in the eighteenth century. The only exception was Dara Shukoh's translations two hundred years ago around 1641. Dara Shukoh was the oldest son of Jahangir, and attracted a liberal courtly crowd of scholars, imperial officers and nobles who followed the eclectic ideology of Akbar. He was a follower of Mullah Mir (d. 1635) and Mullah Shah Badeshi (d. 1661), two important Sufi teachers. He was firmly convinced that the Upanishads preached monotheism, in a similar fashion as did Islam. With the help of Brahmin scholars whom he invited from Benares, he translated fifty two Upanishads and titled the work *Sirr-i-Akbar*. This work traveled all across the continent, and in 1671, a French traveler named Francis Bernier returned to France with a copy of the Persian *Upanishads*, which were translated into Latin by Duperron and titled *Oupnek'hat*. It is not clear if William Jones knew this work when he, with his group of Benares *pandits*, translated the *Isa Upanishads* in 1799. He was assisted in his works by Hindu *pandits*, but none of their names are featured in the published works. In the early years of the nineteenth century, Rammohun, as a result of his familiarity with the officials of the East India Company and the Baptist missionaries, would have known about the works of William Jones and his collaborative use of pandits.[37] The reading domain within which Rammohun worked was already inhabited by European Orientalist scholars. It is almost as if Rammohun was challenging these

---

[34] Susobhan Chandra Sarkar, *On the Bengal Renaissance* (Calcutta, 1979), p. 17.

[35] For more see Bruce Carlisle Robertson, *Raja Rammohun Roy. The Father of Modern India*. (Delhi: Oxford University Press, 1999), pp. 30-31.

[36] *A Defence of Hindoo Theism. In Reply to the Attack of an Advocate for Idolatry in Madras. 1817.* In *The English Works of Raja Rammohun Roy. Part II*, ed. Kalidasa Nag and Debajyoti Burman (Calcutta: Sadharon Brahmo Samaj, 1946), p. 85.

[37] See Robertson's *Raja Rammohun Ray* for more on this; pp. 10-54.

scholars and their lack of acknowledgement of native support. His readers were the same as those of the Orientalist scholars. Here was an instance of a pandit who had turned Orientalist scholar.

Rammohun had a Western readership that was denied to all natives at that time. Native pandits were not referred to by the Western world. What distinguishes Rammohun is the fact that he was also considered to be an expert on the subject of Hinduism by the Western scholars.[38] This is evident if we look at H. Wilson's lecture "Two Lectures on the Religious Practices and Opinions of the Hindus."[39] Wilson was professor of Sanksrit in Oxford and his lecture was an attempt to summarize the popular practices of the Hindus.[40] According to Wilson, it was important to know the existing philosophies and institutions of the Hindus in order to comprehend them; to "overturn their errors we must know what they are."[41] Wilson cited two sources: H. T. Colebrook, who was an authority on the history of the sastras and the philosophical systems,[42] and Rammohun Roy. Rammohun was portrayed as a reformer who was changing the existing decaying systems.[43] Otherwise, Indian scholars were not recognised, and not even Mrityunjay Tarkalankar was seen as an equal by William Carey. In the *Times*, Rammohun's translations also received good reviews:

> It will be recorded as one of the remarkable incidents of the nineteenth century, that a Brahman of respectable rank and strong powers, thoroughly conversant with his own vernacular and classical literature, and almost equally familiar with the learning of the west, should have been the first to transfer into our own language ... an appreciable portion of these works."[44]

---

[38] Ibid., pp. 55-73.

[39] H. Wilson, *Essays and Lectures on the Religions of the Hindus* (New Delhi: APS Reprint, 1976).

[40] Ibid., p.40.

[41] Ibid., p. 40.

[42] H. T. Colebrooke, *Essays on the History, Literature and Religions of Ancient India* (New Delhi: Cosmo Publications, reprint 1977).

[43] Wilson also mentioned Ramacandra Vidyavagis and Prassana Kumar Thakur as examples of the new breed of Hindus; *Essays*, pp. 52-53.

[44] *The Times*. 2 October (1832), Cited in Robertson, *Raja Rammohun Roy*, p. 66.

Rammohun was able to reach out across to a readership that was Western as he was "equally familiar" with the West and with Islamic and Hindu scholarship. It was not hard for him to receive acclaim in the West; Wilhelm Traugott Krug, Schopenhauer and Schelling cited him. Max Mueller wrote that he was "the first who came from East to West, the first to join hands and to complete that world-wide circle through which henceforth, like an electric current, Oriental thought could run to the West and Western thought return to the East."[45] His capacity to understand the needs of his readership made it possible for him to address Western readers. He did not homogenise his readership, being fully aware that an English readership was different from a native one. The notion of the author was a new concept within India, and more so was a native writing to the English in English.

Conclusion.

It would be meaningful to position *The Gospel of Sri Ramakrishna* within this context. Like Rammohun before him, Sri Ramakrishna was also involved in reinterpreting Hinduism at a time period when British colonization of India was at its peak.

---

[45] F. Max Muller, *Biographical Essays* (London, 1884), p. 13.

www.ingramcontent.com/pod-product-compliance
Lightning Source LLC
Chambersburg PA
CBHW041808040426
42449CB00001B/17